Crow Dancing

poetry of the fields, lanes and land

Mandy Whyman

Lavender Button Books

The right of Mandy Whyman to be identified as author of this work has been asserted in accordance with the Copyright, Designs and Patents Act 1988

Copyright © 2022 Mandy Whyman

All rights reserved. This book or any portion thereof may not be reproduced or used in any manner whatsoever without the express written permission of the author.

Cover image: Sonny Mauricio - Unsplash

In memory of Jack and Jean and to Brian and John who all together taught me to love the land.

And Skipper, the dog, who bullies me into going outside even when I don't want to.

Contents

Crow Dancing	9
After the Storm	10
Dance the Year	12
Winter Sunset	14
Snowdrop	15
Shadow Walking	16
Conker	18
High Wind	20
Sowing Seeds	21
After the Storm	22
Byway Blooms	24
Early Spring	26
Song	28
Blackthorn	29
Roadkill	30
Ode to a Fly-Tipper	32
Here	33
Death in The Garden	34
Storm	37

Pretending	38
Harvest Walk	40
Late Summer Rain	42
Bands of Gold	43
Simple	44
Ploughing	46
Clocks Fall Back	47
Fragments	48
December Mist	50
Going	51
For Fun	52
Be Still	53
Poppies	54
Hymn	56
Autumn's Dance	58
The Gate	59
School Run	60
Promises	63

Crow Dancing

Forked footsteps:

Water diviners

Marking the snow –

Slow, slow, quick-quick, slow –

Twisting, turning,

Intersecting…

The trail of a tail

Sashaying behind

In parallel bars.

Black on white.

Piano keys.

Leaving tracks like music notes:

Crow dancing

Trails tracking

The white spread

Of new snow.

After the Storm

The wind waged war
Through the night,
Hurling rain
Like pellets against the panes
And whipping trees and corners
Into howling.

Come morning:
Grey clouds sulk in ragged flags
Against an icy sky
And broken branches litter the road –
Shrapnel of the storm.

Wide puddles lake the lanes,
Ditches dance as gullies,
Gurgling and burbling
In a scatter of storm-news.
My boots skitter diamonds.

The wind, spent,

Flutters the leaf-fall

In little letters

Of truce.

Dance the Year

Corvids claim the year:

Clasp the days in clever claws

And feather nests with time.

Rule the roost from high,

Wind-tossed crow's nests that defy

The Ides of March,

And they "Call-Call-Call"

To arms, in the plundering of the fields

And dark squadrons that wheel

And ward off marauding buzzards.

They strut and steal and mock:

Soundtrack the seasons

In the rattle of the magpie,

The grate of the jay,

The jabber of the jackdaws'

Squabble and gossip,

Home to roost on chimney pots,

And the high pirate cry:

"Caw!" Call to them all

To soar and dance the air:

Black punctuation of the sky –

Question, exclamation, annotation –

Catching wind like dust and leaves and light

On wide-spread wings

Of coal, agate and night.

Thieves and crooks and masters –

They duck and dive and soar through days:

Defy and dance the year.

Winter sunset

Still ice sky

And the low winter sun

Ignites the trees:

Flame!

Dry leaves

Ticker like torches;

Rustling burnished in fire.

The sun blazes

The cold horizon,

Match-striking tree tops

That reach to light

A lantern moon

Snowdrop

Small:

Like first rain,

A pearl of wisdom,

A seed of hope

Against the steel of frost.

White:

Snow-flaked,

Bannering Cold's surrender –

Ringing Spring's bridal bells –

Small clusters of promise:

"This too shall pass," they call

In tiny morse-messages,

White-punctuated

Blooming

Along the winter verge.

Shadow Walking

My long shadow

Dips and trips

Between the sunset trees

Like memory

Caught on burnished branches.

A me; not-me,

Fleeting and fluid,

Pinioned once against a hedge

In paper-doll dimension:

A thread

Sewn,

Woven

Into the fabric

Of trunks and leaves and branches;

The breeze; the breath

The great whole

Of a tiny moment:

The shadow me

Whispered small; tucked

Into the tapestry

Of evening

Conker

Hatching:

Copper hedgehog pods

Spiked and splitting.

Treasure

Lost beneath limbs

That leaf golden

And let go

The trance of Summer.

An imagining of wonder:

Splitting like loaves.

Metamorphosis

Peeks and breaks

Into the warm eye

That blinks, lustrous.

Folded,

Warm as a heart

Into a palm.

Pocketed –

Autumn ingot

High Wind

Wind rolls in waves

On the high-shore tree tops,

Breaching the beach

Of wintered limbs

In the whoosh and shush

Long tumble of rumbling.

Skittish,

Tall branches ticker an answer:

Run, run, run,

And, like a chant

Dry leaves

Flitter, skitter bronzed away

While twigs lose grip

And clatter, chatter alarm

Into the arms of the Wind –

Into the casual cruelty

Of the long rolling

Winter wind.

<u>Sowing seeds</u>

Each one a promise,

A prayer.

Bedded down in earth

Not yet quite warm enough.

Committed to that silent gestation :

Dark and secret.

Magical.

Breathless

Until the small unfurl;

The pushing out of life.

Tender beginnings –

Green and new.

After the Storm

The wind waged war
Through the night,
Hurling rain
Like pellets against the panes
And whipping trees and corners
Into howling.

Come morning:
Grey clouds sulk in ragged flags
Against an icy sky
And broken branches litter the road –
Shrapnel of the storm.

Wide puddles lake the lanes,
Ditches dance as gullies,
Gurgling and burbling
In a scatter of storm-news.
My boots skitter diamonds.

The wind, spent,

Flutters the leaf-fall

In little letters

Of truce.

By-way Blooms

Invasive –

A species almost naturalised

Blooms in clusters

Along ditches and by-way edges:

Sprouts

Without a growing season,

Sown and grown

By passing cars

And their incumbent

Indiscriminate idiots.

Tumbled into hedgerows,

There they grow,

Their fading wrapper paper

Filled with scraps

Of KFC and Maccie D.

Take-away cups bud and proliferate –

Starbucks and Costa genus.

There are more exotics too –

Cans, bottles, Covid-care detritus –

Strange bloomings:

The sowings of throwings.

The careless creeping garden

Of passing.

Passing on.

Passed

Earth – keepers.

Early Spring

The long, wet winter
And tractor tracks have sunk a moat
With high mud bastions
That harden in early Spring
Against the footpath.
The warmth is slow to come,
Besieged by Northern winds
And late frosts….

    Still
Along the embattled hedgerows
White banners of blackthorn burst
Blooms of defiance
And catkins hang tremulous
But steadfast on barren branches.
Blackbirds herald the morning,
Bugling in the forward guard:
The days that creep longer,

Bright fingers tracing green

Across sodden fields and blackened trees.

Victory holds its breath –

Waits to explode.

Held pent and tight in a million furled buds –

Life!

Song

Blackbirds can mimic.

Who'da thought?

That trilling, rilling evensong

Might steal a walker's whistle,

A ringtone,

Maybe me…

Into long evenings

With the twilight creeping

On soft-soled slippers,

Steal me away

From the walls

And calls of commitments.

Mimic me.

Make me; add me too.

A willing hostage found,

Bound in a blackbird's song.

Blackthorn

Cold early Spring:
Bridal, blackthorn throws on
A froth of white,
Trails of lace petal-veiling,
Betraying softened thorns
In a strange marriage
Of frost and beauty.

Too soon the blossoms grey.
Leaves will come
And barbs will show.
The months will yield
The union's bitter fruit –
The slow, bruised berries
Of an early Spring
Deception.

Roadkill

There's a blinkered speed that shapes the ways
Of hardened roads and hearts;
That breaks the necks, the backs, the softened parts –

The sometimes hearts.

Where squirrels and pigeons flatten – become patterned
With the asphalt. Shadows
Of their former selves. Neatly un-creatured.

Where pheasants fling out scattered plumage, somehow
Always with a wing raised, useless, in surrender –

The hearts of small and stupid things.

There
Foxes stretch Dali-esque bright – nose, tail, spine stretching

In frantic, mis-timed flight

Teeth bared to grasp at breath gone silent –

A way not won.

Here

At the asphalt's edge, badgers curl to die;

Seem to sleep.

Black and white pot-holed reminders

Of speedy progress and meetings made.

And the hearts of small and stupid things.

Ode to a Fly-tipper

They're hard to track –

Those that leave a scattered spoor

Of Starbucks cups and sheddings of Maccie-D's.

Just passing through – it's what they do:

Leave their scat in country lanes,

The scant offerings

Of little brains.

They'll be the ones who say

They pay their taxes any-way,

And coffee cups morph to bigger things:

Rubbish, rubble, mattresses and stuff

Spat out in fields and country lanes –

The leavings of those little brains

And a geography that cannot join

Someone else's lanes

To home.

Here

Here. Here.

Find me here

Where the bright-eyed robin

Follows the turning of the earth.

Where the sparrows chatter

In high colours of the morning.

Where the pigeons' low-throated calls

Meld the afternoon

And somewhere high and silent

A kite rides the thermals.

Find me here

Where what is me, is incidental, small

To the wide land; to the wind;

To the life-pulse of calling birds.

Death in the Garden

Death comes to gardens

Nonchalant; silent.

Small things transpire, expire,

Breathe out in an irony

At odds with the Spring.

It is the way it is:

A wandering magpie steals the chicks

And warm eggs fall from nests.

Bees buzz helpless in spider webs

And Nature marches on –

Unflinching.

It is the way it is:

When birds die

When songs end and twig-light toes curl,

Death calls rudely, persistently.

A pigeon caught in the hedge,
Wings spread and soft grey already smelling
Of rot in the sun.
Becomes a small and necessary job –
Digging the hole and covering in earth.

Not so easy the blackbird,
Drowned in an unguarded water butt,
Its fledgling wings weighed heavy
Just below the rim – too low
For escape.

I watched the nest and saw
That brood grow and dart.
Saw them flutter, grow bold, chirp insolence.
Felt a kinship; bond –
Hatched on a shelf in my shed.

The garden seemed silenced

In the silence of that bird.

And when I held it,

Wet feathers, bright eye hooded,

I found I couldn't seal it in solid earth.

I tucked it instead beneath a hedge.

A pretence. Denial. A human weakness.

Nature marched on.

Other blackbirds took up the song.

Storm

I love the light

Against a darkened sky,

When the purple rage of atmosphere

Hangs in backdrop:

An opera waiting.

The whole world –

Trees, leaves, walls, all –

Explodes into light

As if on fire,

Every surface ablaze,

Rippling and beautiful. Bursting.

Cast in bronze and gold –

Emblazoned against the coming storm.

Crescendo!

… and the hammering, insistent drumming

Of rain.

Pretending

Down the Garden Centre
Yarrow is selling
At ten pounds a pot.
I stop to gaup and point:
`Yarrow!'

Down the fields
The yarrow froths the tracks
In background to the bright
Of cornflower, ragwort, scabiosa
And thistles grown tall, majestic, wild.
There, the unexpected blue of chicory,
And sturdy clumps of low clover,
The purple like spears between the white –
In pockets. Like gems.

Back at the Garden Centre:
`Yarrow is a popular perennial'.

It populates the trollies of millennials

Planting cottage gardens in pots on patios….

There is an irony here:

The buying back

Of what once just was.

Disassociation; displacement –

Fake fields of yarrow.

Harvest Walk

There is a silence in the morning,
The long, slow breathing
Of a waking sky
Where the smell
Of earth and cut straw
Lie like honey.

Fields slip fluid away,
Tram lines like arteries
Bleeding into gold
Washing into frothed edges
Of Autumn-overgrown tracks.

Far away mews
Of seagulls trailing a tractor
Beetling the horizon,
Turning the breath-dark earth
In a rhythm of the seasons:
Harvest, promise, harvest.

Life breathes in the almost silence,

Beats in my pulse,

Fills the morning

Under the wakened sky.

Late Summer Rain

The rising wind
Rustles the wheat
Into waves of rumours:
Rain, rain, rain
And grey
Strokes along the horizon,
Drawing down the gauze
Of a million droplets.

A curtain falls,
Blots out the motorway,
Drawing lines in the land:
Battle lines; boundary lines; heart lines.
The wheat shudders, reaches,
Whispers:
"Rain."

Bands of Gold

Morning walk:

The wheat has been cut

And lies in long gilded ridges

Across the fields -

Shards of light above the stubble.

Cut-dust smell

Of warm harvest

Edging the tramlines

In echoes of barns and bedding;

Scents of summers past

Binding

The gilt-stalked wheat.

A vow-renewal,

Man and land intertwined

In long-lying bands of gold.

Simple

No clever innuendo.

No metaphor that extends;

Upends; layers meaning.

This is a simple thing

That bursts the heart open

That lights up eyes and sends the skin tingling:

A simple thing –

This love

That sends the soul soaring

In weightless wonder; One-ness

Love:

The bright white low winter sun

And the mist rolling back through trees and field edges.

The track that glistens, frosted

And the wide, wide sky

And the trees that tremble Autumn

To the sharp kiss of morning air.

Love.

Simple.

Ploughing

A sea:

The tractors navigate

The rich brown surges;

Rolling earth waves

Calling gulls to the turning wake.

A sea, an ocean

Of undulating

Where tender shoots

Will ripple water-green

In the Spring

And shimmer in gold

Lakes of harvest,

Becalmed in the September sun.

The tractors navigate the horizon,

The rich ridges

Of life: this sea; this land.

Clocks fall Back

The clocks fall back

And yesterday's dark is dawn.

Crows float, black cut-outs

Against the pinking sky.

Season changes

Quick-step on the breeze;

Fingertips of October

Slip chill into November's hand,

The wind sighs,

Leaves drop red

Kisses to the ground.

Fragments

When the dawn comes

It is born on gusts of left-over storm

And treads sodden underfoot.

Bouldered beet lies high in piles

As fortress walls edging the field

Against the winter

And a year that slips away, away…

Rolling the wet land and watered sky

To where my footsteps cannot go.

Crows take flight;

Splinter arrows against a blushing sky,

Fragment my heart

Into wind-blown cut-outs that drift

Away, away...

This tongue catches at what words cannot say –

A cipher that tugs out of reach,

Into the wind

And the vast whispering of trees;

The dawn.

The dark, floating, free

Fragments of my heart.

December mist

The mist hangs heavy,

Close to the ground,

Muffling the world

To mere metres,

Marooning the dark December trees -

Alone against the dark.

The world is still and sodden

And small – diminished

To the sound of tread on tarmac

And breath…

Then the sudden rush

Of rooks startled,

Exploding in black shrapnel

To be swallowed by the mist

That hangs heavy

Muffling the world

In my December heart.

Going

Soon I'll be gone,

My feet will walk another route.

I'll be gone

And the paths I know so well

Won't know me anymore.

The track that gives beneath my boots

Will forget my tread.

My muddy prints will wash away…

The trees that lean in

And whisper along the lanes –

They will forget my name,

My voice, my half-articulated dreams.

The hedgerows, the ditches, the furrowed land,

The paths that have led me on

Still will be. Will hold.

But not with memory

Of me.

<u>For fun</u>

The wind picks up

And birds stream in:

Soaring, gliding, scattering

Like leaves

For no apparent reason.

Going nowhere –

The gulls glide, regroup,

And a squadron of jackdaws

Catches at the winds,

Dips against the draft.

Going nowhere –

They play the wind,

Float the upstream,

Bank against the blast –

Going nowhere – just for fun.

Flying

Because they can.

<u>Be still</u>

Beyond the words of war

And waste and loss and lost

And the whine of fragile economics

That clutter the papers, the news,

The views of every chat-show host:

The endless end-of-world,

End-of-days money-grubbing compromises

Made to a planet that un-freezes, bleeds…

Beyond it all, still,

Be still. Stop.

The world turns into Autumn,

Rust licks at the edges of leaves.

Jackdaws jabber into the cooling air.

In some Ecuadorian graveyard

A brand-new snake is found.

The sky turns pink in a familiar miracle

Of morning. Still.

Be still.

Poppies

The poppies bleed out

Across the field - more

Than I've ever seen.

        This will be their last year...

Already the ground is broken

And the earthwork piles of soil

Lie like grave-yard humps;

Bruised borders against the red

Of the poppies that flare

Warning in the morning sun.

The play-god of progress

Has set out little flags -

Jaunty signs of pipework, cables -

The hang-ropes of this field.

And the developers send in the JCBs

Behind wire fences that warn:

"Property of...trespassers will be prosecuted."

Bartered off, birdsong will give way

To the thud and the blood

Of bricks and mortar.

And the poppies will bleed out

And out, with the camomile and hares,

Until all is gone. Bricked over, lost

To memory: a field of poppies

Stained like blood, a flood

Of red weeping in the morning sun

<u>Hymn</u>

Raining. And the drops

Kiss the earth,

Collecting as crystals on leaves,

Pooling a hymn from my memory

- When I look up –

The swallows dart between the rain shards,

Dancing against the sky

- And see in awesome wonder –

They circle like arrows,

Pointers above the field

Where dry wheat wettens into gold

Before my eyes.

- Thy power throughout –

Where the froth of purple

Bursts from thistle-thorned carapace

And suddenly, unlikely,

A hawk so low I can see its eye

Swoops across the field

- Then sings my soul –

And all the world is mine,

Alone and all,

And all

- How great Thou art –

Here in the rain, where the trees tremble

And drops kiss the earth.

Autumn's Dance

Autumn dances

Beneath the shifting ballroom of the sky:

Trees sashay and twirl

In skirts of green, orange, red

And yellow, windfall

Crab apples lie like baubles

In leaves that drop confetti-like –

Discarded dance-cards

Of the Summer done and gone

While Autumn dances on.

The Gate

There is a gate beside the track –

The sort the farmers use –

Not rusted yet, the bolts hang loose

Like severed limbs

And weeds invade wide-ribbed bars.

What was it that it guarded,

Before the fields were bought and built?

Did it corral in the sheep? The cows?

Or keep marauding children from the crops?

Does its metal memory

Recall the swing and grown and clack,

The tractors rumbling route,

The seasons' plough and sow?

Does it long for the hedgerows

Bird song, solitude…

A time not so long ago?

School Run

(Newport to TREA, Penkridge)

The tar courses and slows

Beside the school

Where parents double-park and crowd the pavements,

Then gathers speed

Into roundabouts and past discount stores

Where early-morning shoppers bustle

In a flurry of trolleys and bags.

It undulates and curves away

Past stone walls and cottages

That never meant to be this close to traffic.

It climbs out of the bend

To where hedgerows lap the asphalt edges

And cows linger on the slopes

Like so many sculptures against the light.

Then it is tumbling downhill, towards the Park,

Past the sheep-fields, with woolly dots

Like mushrooms against the islands of autumn copses

And shadows of far-distant hills.

The road broadens, runs straight

Bearing the growing morning traffic ever on.

Two lazy turbines sign the finish line
Like gymnasts tumbling above the treetops.
And, unexpectedly, a V of Canada geese
Arrow across the current
And between the lampposts, out of sight:
Commuters, on the morning run.

Promises

A shepherd's warning:

Red sky in the morning.

But the blaze of pink and blood,

Raise the banner of battle won –

The oncoming of the sun.

Like a blushing bride

Before the veil falls,

And all becomes a promise.

Red sky is the spilling of a heart,

The promise of a start. Restart:

The unfurling of a day,

First bleeding,

Red, bright unpeeling

Of a promise:

Rain – and sun to come.

About the Author

Mandy is a poet and novelist based in Shropshire, England. The granddaughter of a farmer and daughter of a conservationist, she has always loved the land.

Her favourite things are books, plants, trees, wild things - and tea.

This is her fourth collection of poetry. She has also written a novel under the pen name MJ Whyman.

Other works:

<u>Poetry</u>

Whispers from Southern Lands (2019)

Evidence (2019)

Fieldsong (2020)

<u>Novel</u> (MJ Whyman)

Like Water (2022)

www.ingramcontent.com/pod-product-compliance
Lightning Source LLC
Chambersburg PA
CBHW070337120526
44590CB00017B/2918